EMPOWER YOUR FINANCIAL FUTURE

A Woman's Guide to Financial Freedom

CHERESE PENDLETON

AUTHENTIC ENDEAVORS PUBLISHING

AuthenticEndeavors.com

Books may be purchased by contacting the publisher and author at:

Publisher: Authentic Endeavors Publishing
Cover & Interior Design: Teresa Velardi at Authentic Endeavors.
Editor: Teresa Velardi
ISBN: 978-0-9982105-2-0
Library of Congress Control Number: 2018943489

DEDICATION

This book is dedicated to those women who are on their journey to Financial Freedom. Those who are not afraid of the hard work, sacrifice and commitment it takes to build a legacy for their families.

Keep building and remember: YOU ROCK!

CONTENTS

ACKNOWLEDGMENTS

I would like to acknowledge my Lord and Savior Jesus Christ who I keep at the forefront of everything that I do.

To my Mom who has always made sacrifices to ensure that my brothers and I were safe, feed and sheltered. Thank you for always having my back in everything I do or whatever I'm inspiring to be. Love you.

To my sons, Justin and Aaron who have been the reason that I "Go Hard" to set an example for them to follow. You both are smart young men and with commitment and hard work, you can accomplish anything. Thank you for being the inspiration that drives me. LoveUMore

To my brother Greg in heaven, who, when he was on this earth, would motive me through long talks full of laughter and great advice. I will cherish you and those memories forever. Rest in Paradise Brother. See you soon.

To my new friend, Teresa Velardi who has motivated me to push hard to reach my next level of success. I could not have written this book without your help. Thank you for bringing my vision for the book to life.

INTRODUCTION

Through my research of the **gender wealth gap**, defined as the discrepancy in net worth between men and women, I identified many factors that contribute to this inconsistent distribution of wealth. To address these differences, we must investigate practical solutions to bridge the gap.

This book is intended to get you started on your path to implementing strategies and achieving measurable success to plan for a better future. It's time to create the life you want.

Shift your mindset and level up your knowledge about money. Move your thoughts about wealth from "I can't" to "I can." Then you will realize that anything can be done *if* you are committed and willing to make substantive changes and sacrifices.

Many women in the workplace are unaware of the disparity in wages for work performed by men and women. Nor are they aware of the gap in wages faced by different ethnic groups, including African-American and Latina women. The wealth gap is alarming and needs to be addressed, however, keep in mind that wealth begins with your earning potential.

The equal pay conversation is ongoing and probably will be for years to come. This book focuses on principles and strategies to help you attain financial freedom even with the wage gap.

I aspire to spark a new and better conversation regarding the gender wealth gap leading to action and impact. Today, I challenge you to start building your future and the future of your family.

CHAPTER ONE
Establish and Envision Your Life Goals

"You've got to have a vision and an intention and that will guide what you do. I call it devotion. Ask yourself, is this not moving me toward where we need to be? I believe that's helpful because a vision pulls you forward *and it keeps you focused. A vision for the day, for the week, for the month and a lifelong vision - whatever works for you. And then you govern your activities and your behaviors accordingly."*

IYANLA VANZANT

Picture your future! Can you see it vividly? What steps are you taking to get there? Will you even leave something, anything, behind to prove that you even existed?

Whether positive or negative, the choices you make could have an impact on your family. What type of legacy do you want to leave?

Most people want to leave a legacy of some kind, whether it be assets, good values or personal beliefs. Unfortunately, many people are leaving behind an unintended legacy of bad debt. Time is our most precious commodity, and everyone has the same twenty-four hours in a day to get things done. What will you do to make an impact during the next twenty-four hours with your name on them?

When I was twenty years old wondering what life would look like at forty, I blinked, and twenty-five years had flown by. Have you ever felt that way? Does it feel like decades have gone by and you suddenly realize that you're in your forties? I had no idea where the time went. This confirms that we have to maximize our time.

Set Your Goals

> "Setting goals is the first step in turning the invisible into the visible."
>
> Tony Robbins

Are you someone who makes New Year's Resolutions? I'd like to suggest making a list of "Solutions" instead. Let's work on solving the financial issues you may be facing as you close out one year and begin a new, rather than focusing on what didn't get done. Leave what is behind you just where it belongs, in the past.

The first thing to do every year is to establish your short-term and long-term goals. Short-term goals are usually to be completed within six months. Long-term goals are most often set with dates more than six-months or a year out and sometimes up to five or even ten years to complete. Goals must also be **S.M.A.R.T.** **S**pecific **M**easurable **A**ttainable **R**ealistic and **T**imely. See the definitions and examples below.

Goal setting creates a path for you to follow.

> ***A Harvard Business study revealed remarkable statistics relating to goal setting and success. The study found that the 14% who have goals are 10 times more successful than those without goals. The 3% with written goals are 3 times more successful than the 14% with unwritten goals.***

The Harvard Business study identifies writing goals as a key to success. Maybe you're earning enough money to live comfortably but can't find the time to enjoy life. If your goal is to spend more quality time with your family or friends, evaluate what you spend your time on daily.

As you use the worksheet below to develop your **S.M.A.R.T.** goals, you'll understand why it's important to put your goals in writing where you can see them. We can talk about it all day but until we see it in writing we won't see anything to work towards.

One of my goals is to be able to take care of my mother so that she can live comfortably. She's made so many sacrifices for me.

Mom was able to raise her family of three as a single mother and now she is taking care of my grandmother. I am grateful for all she has done for me and my grandmother, so I will do my best to be able to take care of her in return.

WHAT'S YOUR VISION

"Vision without action is merely a dream.
Action without vision just passes the time.
Vision with action can change the world."
JOEL A BARKER

Have you ever created a vision board? A vision board is literally a board on which you display pictures of the things you want in life.

They can represent both short-term and long-term goals. Finding the pictures to put on the boards is fun and will really help you to create even bigger visions for your future.

Vision boards are a great way to document what you want to accomplish for the year. But, it's not worth the board it's created on unless you put your vision board in action! Start building that dream life you've created in your mind and is now visible on the board. Create your beautiful, powerful board and put it on display in a place where you will see it multiple times throughout your day. Putting it under your bed or in your closet is NOT an option.

"If you don't have a vision, you're going to be stuck in what you know. And the only thing you know is what you've already seen."

Iyanla Vanzant

Work for your vision ... You've just created a roadmap to achieve your goals. Revisit your board each month. Identify what you have already achieved, keep your eye on what you are about to achieve, and keep aiming high for the things that are just over the horizon.

Get excited about what you have done so far and what is just around the corner!

Positivity is Key

"You are the average of the five people you spend the most time with."

Jim Rohn

Surround yourself with positive people and share your goals with them. Set your intention and talk about the possibilities ahead. Encourage them to be part of your vision.

Your girlfriends will understand and appreciate why you said NO to going on a shopping spree with them. Better yet, surround yourself with like-minded people who are working towards the same goals you are. Support and accountability will help you work towards your goals quicker. Say "No" to the Naysayers.

Creating S.M.A.R.T. Goals*

A **S.M.A.R.T**. Goal is defined as one that is specific, measurable, attainable, realistic, and timely.

Specific: Goals should be simplistically written and clearly define what you are going to do. This is the Who, What, Where, When,

Why, and Which of the S.M.A.R.T. model.

Example: "By January 15, 2018, set up a direct deposit with my payroll representative to automatically transfer $100 to my savings account every two weeks."

Measurable: Goals should be measurable so that you have concrete evidence that you have accomplished the goal. Some questions to consider when thinking about the measurability of the goal – How much, How many, and how will I know when it's accomplished.

Attainable: Goals should be attainable; they should stretch you so you feel challenged, but defined well enough so that you can achieve them. It requires time and research to see if this goal is actually something that is possible for you to do.

Realistic: Goals must represent an objective towards which you are willing and able to work. Ask yourself if the goal is representative of what you really want and the direction in which your life is going?

Timely: Goals should be linked to a timeframe that creates a practical sense of urgency, or results in tension between the current reality and the vision of the goal. Without such tension, the goal is unlikely to produce a relevant outcome. If you want to join a fitness studio, when do you want to join by? "This year" won't work.

Go to the Chapter Check-Ups section and review the S.M.A.R.T. Goals Worksheet/Questionnaire*

* S.M.A.R.T. Goals documents adapted from those found at http://www.hr.virginia.edu

CHAPTER TWO
Create Multiple Sources of Income

"The best decision I ever made was when I just committed myself to really learning how to be a good entrepreneur."
DR. BOYCE WATKINS

IT'S NO LONGER A NINE-TO-FIVE WORLD

Have you been struck by the reality that your salary isn't enough to pay your every day bills and pay off your debt? It may be time to consider ways to supplement your income. Have you ever thought about a side hustle to help pay down the debt? Would you like to earn extra money to save for that much needed vacation? Wouldn't it be nice to have more money to add to your retirement savings? The question that you should be asking yourself is, "What happens if your job decides to quit YOU?"

While I was working for a well-known finance company, I felt so bad for my co-worker who told me it was her 18th anniversary with the company and she didn't receive recognition from anyone. Eighteen years with the company and... nothing. I would think Human Resources would have recognized her long-term service with the company on her anniversary. Maybe that responsibility falls on shoulders of the supervisor, if you have a good one. There are many people in higher positions that shouldn't be managing people. Apparently, my supervisor thought it necessary to constantly remind of the efficiency of robots and how easily they would be able to do my job. Imagine that. So much for "Human" resources!

A 2017 report in MarketWatch found that half of American households currently live paycheck to paycheck.

Outside of your day to day work, your nine to five, there are probably tasks you do daily for someone that you could be monetizing. Just think of how awesome it would be to use your skills and talents in your own business.

There's always the "flip" industry. Powerhouse platforms like Amazon or eBay could be a place to start selling your goods. The beauty of selling nowadays is that you don't have to just sell locally. Yes, there are platforms like "Offer-up" and "Let-go" where you can advertise items you are selling locally, and there are millions of potential customers reachable through the assistance of the internet.

"Our grandparents didn't have the options we have, we live in a 24/7 world - you can make money in your underpants when you get back home from your waitress job."

GARY VAYNERCHUK

ARE YOU AN ENTREPRENEUR

Entrepreneurship has always been in my blood. I remember when my brothers and I were very young we had a paper route that my Mom helped us with. We didn't even have a car to make the deliveries! Back in those days it was freezing cold in the winter. By the time we would finish the route our fingers felt as frozen as icicles. The Sunday paper was thick and heavy... and, oh no... don't let it rain! We never wanted any complaints of wet newspapers from our customers. What a great lesson my Mom taught us at such a young age. We learned to handle money, and were skilled in time management, and customer service. All these skills I learned before becoming a teenager are always at my service.

After my rewarding real estate career, I started working with a coach to strategize my next career move. With the help of that coach, I finally became clear on what I needed to do to fulfill my life's purpose.

Is this the time to step out into the world as an entrepreneur? I encourage you to find your passion... discover what you love doing and who it would benefit, then... Go For IT!

Take a moment to go through the worksheet in the Chapter Check Up Section. It will help you uncover some golden nuggets of who you are, what you bring to the world, how you can make a difference for others and in the end, create an increase in your income. This may be the birth of the entrepreneur in you.

CHAPTER THREE
Evaluate Your Debt
Who You Owe?

"The rich rules over the poor, and the borrower is the slave of the lender."
PROVERBS 22:7

It's time to look at your overall debt. How much money do you owe? Who do you owe that money to? I know this is someplace where you might not want to go, so before we broach this increasingly sensitive subject let's define debt.

GOOD DEBT

Good debt is the debt that is working to make money for you.

> ***According to money.howstuffworks.com: Good debt is an investment that will grow in value or generate long-term income.***

Taking out student loans to pay for a college education is an example of good debt. However, in this changing economy, many people are in serious financial trouble with student loan debt right now. Be sure to research and plan carefully so that you don't end up wasting money on student loans. You may not be able to find a good job in your field of study to pay it back.

A mortgage is a great example of good debt since the value of your house is appreciating over time as the amount of money you owe is decreasing over time and creating equity in the property. Investing in your own business is another example of good debt. It will increase the value of your business creating a greater bottom line for the business, more income for you and your family and increasing the overall monetary value of the company.

Bad Debt

Bad debt is the debt that is costing you money

> ***According to investinganswers.com: In business, bad debt is the portion of a loan or portfolio of loans a lender considers to be uncollectable. In personal finance, bad debt generally refers to high-interest consumer debt.***

More importantly, we need to focus on bad debt, the debt that is costing you money. Credit cards are the first on the bad debt list. Most people use credit cards to purchase things that depreciate (lose their value) rapidly while the accrued interest adds to the balance you actually owe.

> ***According to their analysis of 2016 credit card debt trends, in a recent report, WalletHub.com, a personal finance site reported these findings: When it comes to individual households, the average American family owes $8,377.***

Knowing exactly how much you owe is important to assess your financial shape. When I worked as a Banker, one of my clients came in the branch every month to pay down a credit card that her late husband opened in her name without her permission. In fact, he opened two cards and charged $25k total. She didn't find out about the debt until the day she opened the bill. It's a sad day when you discover that can't even trust your spouse with your financial wellbeing. I had no idea things like this happen until I heard my client's story.

Because of my client's circumstance, I'm led to believe that it's not uncommon for married couples to have one person handle the household finances. Ladies, since this book is written specifically with you in mind, listen up. Whether you are in a one income household as a single woman, or are married and have two incomes creating your financial picture, or if you are married and there is one income, *know your financial situation*! I can't stress this enough. I implore you, don't become the woman who walked into the bank having to pay off money she didn't even know she owed.

> "I vowed never again to create more bills than I could pay. I just hated the way overspending made me feel. Why anyone chooses to live a life in debt has always been a puzzle to me."
>
> OPRAH WINFREY

That example is exactly why it's important to order a FREE copy of your credit report each year. There are three credit reporting agencies that track the health of your overall credit to determine what's known as a FICO score, which is used to determine your credit worthiness. Each of these agencies, TransUnion, Equifax and Experian will, at your annual request, give you a copy of your credit report free of charge.

There are also websites that monitor your score for you and send you a monthly update. Knowing this information on a regular basis will keep you aware of the status of ALL accounts in your name. This frequent review will alert you as soon as possible of anything on your report pointing to identity theft, which is a HUGE issue in today's digital world.

It's also a good idea to check the interest rates on your credit cards and reach out to those companies to renegotiate if your rates are too high. Credit card companies want your business, and most are willing to make adjustments to your rates if you have a good payment history and are maintaining a good FICO score.

You may also have an introductory rate that is going to expire. Some of those intro rates will increase the interest rate and apply it to the balance you owe, but some, if the balance is not paid by a specified time, will go back and charge the interest on the full amount of the original purchase.

I remember when I needed tires for my car. After price matching, like I always do, I decided to go with the retailer that had what looked like a good offer. The offer was 0% financing for two years. I decided to apply for the offer and set up monthly payments of what I could afford at that time. What a mistake!

Although the payments were timely made, I should have increased the amount each month. I even ignored the reminder I set to pay the balance in full once the introductory period expired. I didn't understand at the time that the entire two years of finance charges would be billed after the introductory period expired. It's all in the fine print. The finance charges ended up being about $300! Can you say, "Lesson learned?"

Seeing your total debt in writing could be your motivation to become debt free. So, let's take a look at how much you actually owe. Good debt and bad debt.

Go to the Chapter Check-Up page for Chapter Three and
List your debt – How much do you owe on each of your accounts? What is the monthly payment and the interest rate on each of the accounts. This information will also be needed when we set up your monthly finances (budget) in the next chapter.

"Knowing is not enough, you must take action!"

TONY ROBBINS

CHAPTER FOUR
Create a Monthly Financial Plan

"It's impossible to map out a route to your destination if you don't know where you are starting from."
SUZE ORMAN

WELCOME TO THE FINE ART OF BUDGETING

A monthly financial plan, aka monthly budget, is a great multi-purpose tool to use for managing your money. Budgeting for the purposes of spending control and building savings to achieve your short and long-term goals will build your confidence in the way you handle your money overall.

A Gallup poll found only about one third of Americans(32%) maintain a household budget.

Creating your budget will shed light on several key areas of your finances. It will give you a starting point as you move forward on your path of wealth creation.

- Do you know really what are you spending your money on?
- How much money do you need to live comfortably now?

- Your bank statements are a pretty good indication of what you care about the most.
- How much are you willing to spend on things that are important to you?
- Is how you are managing your money today the way to be able to get what you want tomorrow?

Although budgeting can be a tedious task, it's worth the sacrifice in the end. Have you ever been irritated by the person in line at the grocery store that pulls out about twenty coupons? It takes discipline and patience to find those coupons, then remember to take them to the store and present them to the cashier. Seeing a real savings on your grocery bill is the reward.

I always do my best to price match the item I am wanting to buy online before making any large purchases. Lately, I've been asking myself, "Is this a want or a need?" Buying impulsively can drain your bank account or run up your credit card balance very fast. Think before you buy! I believe most people, like myself, own a lot of "stuff" they don't need. Some things might still be in the original wrapper and some have never been used. Are you raising your hand to acknowledge that you may be one of those people? I know I am.

It's time for change! I am working towards becoming a minimalist. Less is always more. I feel so much better mentally when my surroundings are clutter free. Being organized also saves time, increases productivity and creates less stress and an overall sense of peace. There are lots of advantages to creating order in our lives.

Let's Get To It

Create a monthly financial plan and develop a strategy to reduce your debt. This will help you to take control of your money. Taking control of your money will overflow into managing other areas of your life.

The following three pages contain images of the Monthly Financial Worksheet I have created for you. They will help you realize all the areas where you are spending your hard- earned dollars. Keeping a watchful eye on your monthly finances (budgeting) lets you decide how to manage your money. The 50/30/20 "budget" suggests you divide your monthly income as follows:

50% is allocated for your "needs," 30% goes toward your "wants," and the remaining 20% is designated for savings and debt repayment.

This worksheet will allow you to keep close track of your monthly finances. By using this method for at least two to three months, you will be able to see exactly where you are spending your money, make adjustments where necessary and create a plan that you can live with on a monthly basis while working your way toward your goals.

Copies of this three-page Monthly Financial Worksheet are available for you to download at: bit.ly/springfinances18

Manage your money before your money manages you!

Finances for the month of ______

Category	Monthly Budget	Monthly Actual	Difference	Notes
Income				
Monthly pay (after taxes)				
Other Income				
Other income				
Total Monthly Income				
Expenses: Housing				
Mortgage or rent				
Real estate property tax				
Homeowner's association or condo fees				
Homeowner's or renter's insurance				
Other				
Total Housing Expenses				
Expenses: Utilities				
Electric				
Gas/heating oil				
Water/sewage				
Internet provider				
Cell phone				
Cable TV				
Other				
Total Utilities Expenses				

Continued on next page

Category	Monthly Budget	Monthly Actual	Difference	Notes
Expenses: Food and Entertainment				
Groceries				
Meals out				
Entertainment (movies, etc.)				
Other				
Other				
Total Food and Entertainment				
Expenses: Children				
Child care				
School tuition				
Lunch money				
School supplies				
Lessons/sports				
Other				
Other				
Total Children Expenses				
Expenses: Personal				
Dry cleaning/laundry				
Personal grooming				
Other				
Other				
Total Personal Expenses				
Expenses: Savings/Large Expenses *Expenses you can budget for, so you have money saved to pay for unplanned or annual bills.				
Savings amount going into an account each month				
Gifts (holiday, birthday)*				
House maintenance/ repairs*				
Church/charity*				
Vacation*				
Other				
Total Savings/Large Expenses				

Total Monthly Income				
Total Monthly Expenses				
Difference				

Category	Monthly Budget	Monthly Actual	Difference	Notes
Expenses: Health/Medical *Expenses that you can budget for, so you have money saved to pay for unplanned or annual bills.				
Medical insurance				
Dental insurance				
Doctor*				
Dentist*				
Orthodontist*				
Therapist*				
Ophthalmologist				
Medicines*				
Other				
Other				
Total Health/Medical Expenses				
Expenses: Transportation *Expenses you can budget for, so you have money saved to pay for unplanned or annual bills.				
Car payments				
Car insurance				
Car maintenance/repair*				
Mass transit costs				
Gas				
Parking/tolls				
Tags/inspection*				
Total Transportation Expenses				
Expenses: Credit Cards, Loans				
Credit Card: Balance:				
Credit Card: Balance:				
Credit Card: Balance:				
Student Loans				
Other				
Other				
Total Credit Card/Loan/ Other Balances and Fees				

Continued on next page

CHAPTER FIVE
Savings/Emergency Fund

"Do not leave yourself or your family unprotected against financial storms....Build up savings."
EZRA TAFT BENSON

SET YOURSELF UP FOR FINANCIAL SUCCESS ESPECIALLY IN AN EMERGENCY

In today's world of click-and-watch-it-show-up-at-your-doorstep, our "wants" are most likely winning over our "needs." Free two-day shipping can be a blessing and a curse. When you need a last-minute gift, it's a blessing. When you keep buying things you don't need just because they are on sale or that you just want to have, you can easily dissolve any notion of having a well-funded savings account! It's that simple.

Curbing your spending is as easy as 1-2-3.

1. Commit to not spending money on anything you don't need.
2. Add the cost of that item to your savings account instead.
3. Commit to putting 10% of your paycheck in the bank every pay period.

Most financial advisors suggest saving 3-6 months of income for emergencies.

How is your savings account looking? Have you saved even $400 or more for emergencies?

> ***As recently as 2016, the Federal Reserve surveyed more than 5,000 Americans about their financial situation. Among the findings was one startling statistic: Approximately 46% of Americans stated they do not have enough money to cover a $400 emergency expense.***

USE WHAT YOU KNOW

Now that you have created a budget it's easier to designate a monthly savings goal. I was always told that we should be paying ourselves first. Saving 10% each pay period will quickly fund an emergency fund. There is really no great advantage to keeping large amounts of money in a savings account. Most people do like to have quick access to their money and think that saving accounts are safer than investing.

One of my customers from the bank came in the branch in a panic one day. She was a very sweet lady, probably in her early 60s with a heavy New York accent. I had arranged for one of my financial partners to help her earn more money from the $50K she had sitting in her savings account. The financial advisor left a detailed message about meeting him to discuss investment options. What I didn't know is that she had kept the account a secret from her husband. Good for her for saving that much money not so sure it's good to keep it from the husband.

I believe that saving money can be done easily through sacrifice. I found that setting up an automatic transfer from my paycheck worked well to help me achieve my savings goal.

“In terms of my profession,
I'm passionate about financial literacy.
I want to live in a financially literate society.
I want kids to understand the importance of
savings and investing. I want to try to
replicate the great savers who came out of the
Depression, the best savers the country has ever seen.
It's crucial that people understand the importance of
financial literacy, because it's actually lifesaving.”
MELLODY HOBSON

LET'S SET SOME SAVINGS GOALS

Go to the Chapter Check-Up in the back of the book and complete the worksheet.

CHAPTER SIX
Investments

"I know many members of our community steer clear of Wall Street because of the perception that the stock market is risky, but I am convinced the biggest risk of all is not taking one."
Mellody Hobson

Are you investing some of your hard-earned money for your future or the future of your family?

Are you confident in those investments?

Do you want to always be working for your money or do you want your money to work for you?

Have you thought about learning how to diversify your investment portfolio?

These are just a few questions to ask yourself about developing your financial future.

The Gender wealth gap is even more concerning than the wage gap. Ladies, we need to shift our money mindset. I don't know about you, but I get excited about educating myself about money and my financial future.

For some reason women haven't been taught about using money as a tool for financial freedom.

Just 43% of women said they were confident in their investments compared to 56% of men in a new study from Financial Finesse.

Of course, there is an element of risk to all investments and that's the most important reason why we need to educate ourselves. What works for one person may not work so well for you.

Your plan must be customized to your individual needs, comfort and goals. We should always be thinking of how to up level our thinking, not our lifestyle.

The Jones' may not be living the lifestyle you think they are. Those fancy clothes, big house, new cars and vacations could be putting them up to their eyes in debt and heading the Jones' for the poor house.

Not everything is as it may seem, however, with education and planning, those things could be in your future without so much debt. Financial freedom can be on your horizon if you really want it. You're never too young or too old to start learning how to invest.

REAL ESTATE

Some people might say you shouldn't consider your home as an investment because of the economic crash of the real estate market in 2008. There are lots of factors to consider, but owning a home is more advantageous than renting. We all have to live somewhere, right? I'm pretty sure that your landlord is not going to allow you the advantage of the tax benefit they are getting from owning that home.

When I sold real estate, my friend hired me to sell her house. She had enough equity to make a profit from the sale. Suppose she had rented that house for 10 years instead. I don't think her landlord would have given her any money for moving out. Investing in a rental property is where it's at. Wouldn't be nice to own a property where you could benefit from someone else paying the mortgage?

DIVERSIFY

My mother always says, "Never put all your eggs in one basket." If this is the rule you live by, diversifying your assets is a good idea to help achieve your financial goals.

According to the Financial Industry Regulatory Authority, (FINRA.org) here are some ways to diversify your investment dollars.

- Bank Products - Banks and credit unions can provide a safe and convenient way to accumulate savings.
- Stocks - When you buy shares of a company's stock, you own a piece of that company.
- Bonds - A bond is a loan an investor makes to an organization in exchange for interest payments over a specified term plus repayment of principal at the bond's maturity date.

- Investment funds - Funds—such as mutual funds, closed-end funds and exchange-traded funds—pool money from many investors and invest it according to a specific investment strategy.
- Annuities - An annuity is a contract between you and an insurance company, in which the company promises to make periodic payments, either starting immediately—called an immediate annuity—or at some future time—a deferred annuity.
- Insurance - Life insurance products come in various forms, including term life, whole life and universal life policies.
- Retirement - Numerous types of investments come into play when saving for retirement and managing income once you retire. For saving, tax-advantaged retirement options such as a 401(k) or an IRA can be a smart choice.

Power of Attorney and Your Investments

It's important to consider how you want your financial affairs to be managed if something happens to you. A power of attorney is a legal document you sign to grant someone you trust the authority to make decisions on your behalf.

Designate someone you trust to act in your best interest as a POA in the event you are unable to make those decisions yourself.

Be sure to contact your attorney for advice on how to best legally protect your assets.

CHAPTER SEVEN
Have a Retirement Plan

"Take free money. No matter how in debt you are, if your employer offers a matching contribution on a 401(k) or other retirement vehicle, you must sign up and contribute enough to get the maximum company match each year. Think of it as a bonus."

SUZE ORMAN

What does retirement look like for you? Do you have a plan in place? Maybe you think you're too young to start planning for retirement. The truth is, you're never too young to begin planning for retirement. Do you think you will have to depend on social security only?

A 2014 report from the Social Security program that estimated that the trust fund reserves will run out in 2034. That means Social Security won't be able to pay full retirement benefits starting in 2033.

Whether or not that's true, the truth is...that's only 16 years from now. Personally, I'll do my best to be sure that my "golden years" are able to be enjoyable with or without the benefit of Social Security.

Relying on the three traditional sources of retirement income (pension, Social Security, and personal savings) is no longer enough.

Many people must find employment after retiring from their job. I can't imagine being sixty-five and having to look for a job.

In today's world of so many jobs being done with technology, it's tough enough to get hired at forty-five. My mother retired at the age of sixty-two. Her challenge is, she still has a mortgage that needs to be paid every month, and like many women, she is now my Grandmother's caregiver, which limits the option of working a job.

It's so funny… when I talk to people about retirement one response I get often is "I'll never be able to retire." Really? Your mindset about anything is a deciding factor in whatever happens in your life. Henry Ford, founder of Ford Motor Company famously said,

> "Whether you think you can or you think you can't, either way, you're right!"
> Henry Ford

Let's be more in a "show me how" mindset. We should make retirement planning a priority and educate ourselves so that when we are at the age to retire we wouldn't be worrying about how.

I recommend taking a moment to understand the basics of the different types of retirement savings accounts and investment vehicles. A financial advisor or financial coach will be able to assist you in designing a plan that is tailored to meet your specific retirement goals.

What age would you like to retire and how money much do you need to retire?

Consider some of the following vehicles as you develop your plan.

- Retirement accounts
- Dividends from stocks
- Social Security
- Personal Savings
- Small Business income
- Real Estate Investment Income
- IRA or 401K Income

Here are two good resources to review to start the retirement conversation.

- https://www.nerdwallet.com/blog/investing/best-retirement-plans-for-you/
- https://www.bankrate.com/calculators/index-of-retirement-calculators.aspx

Go to the Chapter 7 Check-Up page where you can list any accounts/vehicles you have in place for your future retirement.

CHAPTER EIGHT
Life Insurance

"IF THERE IS ANYONE DEPENDENT ON YOUR INCOME – PARENTS, CHILDREN, RELATIVES – YOU NEED LIFE INSURANCE."

SUZE ORMAN

A life insurance policy can be used to protect the savings account you've scarified to build and other assets you have accumulated.

> ***LIMRA's (Life Insurance and Market Research Association) Household Trends in U.S. Life Insurance Ownership revealed that one in five households with children under age 18 are uninsured, according to the 2016 study.***

Do you own a life insurance policy?

What type of policy do you have?

Do you have enough coverage?

There is an old saying that is so true: **Life insurance is for the living not the dead.**

It's important to know exactly what you have. I sold life insurance for several carriers a few years ago. I met a lady who had been making her premium payments on her policy faithfully for nineteen years. For all those years she thought she owned a whole life policy. I wanted to cry the moment I told her that she owned an accidental death policy.

The only way her family could get paid the face amount of the policy was if the cause of death was an accident. She paid $30 a month for NINETEEN years. You do the math!!!

That's one of the reasons why I decided to change careers. I was finding that lots of people were in the same boat. Delivering the news became too emotional for me.

Dying is not an easy subject to talk about. In fact, life insurance was the hardest thing I had to sell. My brother just recently passed away leaving his wife a widow at thirty-nine years young.

Unfortunately, he didn't own a life insurance policy. Not only were we dealing with the shock of his sudden death, we were dealing with the fact that he didn't own a policy that would even cover final expenses. We had to come up with a plan to pay for the funeral arrangements.

A properly managed financial portfolio should include enough life insurance to replace the insured's income for at least the number of years the surviving parent will be raising the children. When my brother died so suddenly, there was nothing to replace the income he contributed to maintain the lifestyle of his family.

Many people are under the impression that they don't have to buy an individual policy because they have insurance at work. We shouldn't just have a policy that is tied to your benefit package with your employer. What happens if you lose that job? Your policy may be able to transfer; however, it may cost more to take it with you. Have a policy outside of what you have that is tied to your job.

I highly suggest you check all policies to ensure you understand exactly what you own. It's not just about leaving the burden of the burial expenses on your loved ones but more importantly, a properly thought out life insurance purchase can support your family for years to come because your planning included leaving a legacy.

Key points to remember when considering the purchase of life insurance:

- The older you get, the higher the cost.
- Smokers pay considerably higher rates for insurance.
- Your health is the greatest factor considered by companies when underwriting (deciding whether you qualify) your application for life insurance.
- Although insurance is highly regulated by state insurance departments, costs and policy options vary from company to company.

Do your "homework" to be sure you know what you are purchasing.

Go the Chapter Check-Up section of the book and record your current life insurance policy information.

CHAPTER NINE
Your Living Will and Last Will & Testament

"Family is not an important thing. It's everything."
MICHAEL J. FOX

Have you prepared for your family's future?

Before we begin, let's define "Living Will" and "Will."

USLegal.com defines a "Living Will" as:

> ***A Living Will is a document that allows a person to explain in writing which medical treatment he or she does or does not want during a terminal illness. A terminal illness is a fatal illness that leads ultimately to death.***

According to Wikipedia, a *"Will"* is defined as:

> ***A Will or Testament is a legal document by which a person, the testator, expresses their wishes as to how their property is to be distributed at death, and names one or more persons, the executor, to manage the estate until its final distribution.***

Here are some very pertinent questions to ask yourself as we broach this sensitive topic:

- Who do you want to decide your fate or the fate of your family?

- Who do you want to take care of your children if something happens that leaves you incapacitated, incompetent or unable, for whatever reason, to make that decision?

I assure you, the last thing you would want to happen is have your assets tangled up in a lengthy probate process.

I just found out that in the state of Virginia, because I'm not married, my twenty-seven-year-old son would be responsible for making health care decisions for me. I'm not so sure that would be the best thing for either of us, should that situation present itself.

My cousin made a great decision by being proactive and creating a living will for her mother. Within six months of creating the documents, her mother had a stroke and because she had those documents in place, it made it easier to handle her mother's healthcare and finances.

> "Make a living will. Talk about it. Death is going to happen to everybody. Write it down. Even if you write it on a piece of paper at home and have your family witness it, you need to write it down."
>
> MICHAEL SCHIAVO

Appoint a health care proxy or power of attorney in writing, with the proper documents, to express your wishes in the event you are not able to speak for yourself due to incapacitation by injury or progressive illness.

Choose someone you can trust to be your voice who will not allow their emotional connection to you get in the way of making good decisions on your behalf.

Consult your attorney for legal advice on your individual needs on health care proxy and power of attorney.

From my experiences while working in the banking industry, I've learned that one of the most important things, and I suggest you do this ASAP, is to have your beneficiary or someone you trust become a co-owner or an authorized user/signer on your bank accounts. I remember how complex the bank's estate process was.

Having to deliver the news to the families of deceased account holders that they had no access to their loved one's funds was heart breaking. Sometimes it could take weeks to have the necessary paperwork completed to gain access to the money. It's so critical to have these tough, but necessary conversations with our family members.

There is great sacrifice made in the process of saving to create a legacy. Making sure you have the proper legal documents in place can keep it from being squandered by the next generation or the one to follow. There are also many ways to make sure everything happens to fulfill your legacy plan.

I can't impress upon you enough the importance of making sure you've taken the necessary steps to substantiate your legacy.

Go to the Chapter Check-Up page where you can answer some pointed questions about your personal planning and record the pertinent information relative to your Living Will and Last Will and Testament.

CHAPTER TEN

Health Check-Up
Mind, Body and Soul

"An empty lantern provides no light. Self-care is the fuel that allows your light to shine brightly."
UNKNOWN

Most financial and estate plans address only the financial dimension of wealth. Wealth is not just about money. The three dimensions of wealth are:

- Financial (net worth, investment),
- Personal (health, personal development) and
- Social (Relationships).

"Being a healthy woman isn't about getting on a scale or measuring your waistline. We need to start focusing on what matters, on how we feel and how we feel about ourselves."
MICHELLE OBAMA

In the previous chapters, we've had a great deal of conversation about developing your financial wealth. Now, let's look at the other two of the three dimensions of wealth.

Personal Wealth

Always remember, **your health *is* your wealth**. In today's environment, it is wise to approach your physical and mental health in the same manner or with even more passion and diligence than you manage your finances.

Are you paying attention to your body? It's important to map out a health plan with your primary physician. When having a conversation with a doctor, it is of great importance to talk about your family history and your daily activities that affect your health. It is our individual responsibility to take care of our bodies and to keep our health care professionals up to date and aware of changes in our personal wellness.

Create a plan of action that will keep you physically healthy. It's been my experience that adding in some positive practices that will keep stress at bay are just as important as regular visits to the doctor.

Meditation and Mindfulness

Through *meditation,* we can discover a fascinating sense of calmness and inner harmony as well as a *way* to help reduce the stress of everyday life. One of the primary benefits of meditation is mindfulness.

Mindfulness is defined as a state of active, open attention on the present. Staying in the present moment helps us to let go of the past, and any mistakes or challenges that we tend to bring into our day to day living. It also keeps us from the busy-ness of planning the future... for the moment anyway. Although planning for the future is important, it can also be overwhelming and stressful.

During meditation, allow yourself, body, mind and spirit to just be in the present moment. Sometimes, through this practice, ideas we may never have thought of while our minds are "busy" come to the surface in the quiet space of meditation.

If you've not yet experienced meditation, give yourself the gift of doing something new. There are many ways to begin. My suggestion would be to go to "YouTube University" and explore what's there. It may be as simple as giving yourself permission to rest for a moment.

There may be times when we may need a boost of confidence to feel better about ourselves. Maybe making simple changes to our appearance will give us that boost.

When was the last time you changed your hairstyle, or bought yourself a new outfit? I would recommend that you budget for whatever is going to help improve your self-confidence.

If you were to look through my photo albums, you wouldn't see many pictures of me when I was in my twenties. My self-esteem was quite low during those years. I didn't like my smile; therefore, I avoided the camera at all costs.

To the people who say, "money can't buy confidence," let me tell you, my confidence had a major boost after my Invisalign treatment. I've spent thousands of dollars and what a huge difference it's made for me. Today, my confidence is much higher, my smile is much brighter, and I'm no longer afraid of the camera.

Let's touch on personal development for a moment.

According to Wikipedia,

> ***"Personal development covers activities that improve awareness and identity, develop talents and potential, build human capital and facilitate employability, enhance the quality of life and contribute to the realization of dreams and aspirations. Personal development takes place over the course of a person's entire life. Not limited to self- help, the concept involves formal and informal activities for developing others in roles such as teacher, guide, counselor, manager, life coach or mentor."***

There is a multitude of personal development programs available today.

Social Wealth

There is value and leverage in having meaningful relationships. Take time to evaluate your current circle of friends and business associates. Are they healthy or unhealthy relationships?

Motivational speaker, Jim Rohn, famously said,

> *"We are the average of the five people we spend the most time with."*
>
> Jim Rohn

Take inventory and decide who, is in your life for a lifetime, reason or season. Personally, I had to cut off a few people to keep my sanity and become my best self. It's time to level up your circle.

Be Discerning

Beware... just because someone is in your circle, doesn't mean they are in your corner.

Surround yourself with people who will lift you up and not drag you down. When we hold each other high, together we can create relationships that have greater depth. There's a peace in knowing that people stand for you and have your back.

Go to the Chapter Check-Up and fill in the pertinent information relative to your health.

CHAPTER CHECK-UPS

This section is designated for you to complete the work outlined in each chapter.

Be as thorough as possible with each section.

Some tips:

- Where you are asked to list accounts, be sure to have the name of the institution where the account is, the current balance and any beneficiary information that may be relative to that account or policy.
- For the inventory of personal effects and or funds to be distributed to beneficiaries by your estate executor, use the "NOTES" pages in the back of the book. Be as thorough as possible.
- Any additional information relative to the Chapter Check-ups can be added to the "NOTES" section as well.
- Once you have completed the work, store this book, with all the information completed in a safe place. Be sure to tell your most trusted person where it is.
- Update the information annually.

Chapter 1
Establish Your Life Goals

What are your top five life goals?

Goal 1

Deadline

Budget

....

Goal 2

Deadline

Budget

....

Goal 3

Deadline

Budget

....

Goal 4

Deadline

Budget

....

Goal 5

Deadline

Budget

....

S.M.A.R.T. Goal Worksheet

The questions following each aspect of S.M.A.R.T. goal setting will help you to better create goals in all aspects of your life. Use the questions to prompt and practice better goalsetting.

Current Goal: ______________________________

____

1. **S**pecific:

- What will the goal accomplish?
- How and why will it be accomplished?

2. **M**easurable.

- How will you measure whether or not the goal has been reached (list at least two indicators)?

3. **A**ttainable.

- Is it possible?

- Have others done it successfully?
- Do you have the necessary knowledge, skills, abilities, and resources to accomplish the goal?
- Will meeting the goal challenge you without defeating you?

4. **R**ealistic.

- What is the reason, purpose, or benefit of accomplishing the goal?

  ____

  ____

- What is the result (not activities leading up to the result) of the goal?

  ____

  ____

5. **T**imely.

- What is the established completion date and does that completion date create a practical sense of urgency?

  ____

  ____

Revised Goal:

____

____

____

How do you manage your time?

Do you have a Daily Calendar set up in a digital format like Google or Outlook?
Or do you have a printed Daily Planner?

How do you spend most of your time?

____

____

How many hours do you sleep?

____

How many hours is your commute?

____

How many hours a day do you work?

____

How many hours a day to you relax?

____

Bring Your Vision to Life

What is the vision you have for your life?

____

____

____

____

____

____

____

____

If money was no object, what would you be doing?

CHAPTER TWO:
CREATE MULTIPLE SOURCES OF INCOME

First, what are your gifts?

These are the skills and talents that come easily to you. They are the gifts you were born with. List them here... all of them.

What do you do for fun that you could be being paid for?

Next, let's look at what you would like to create to make your financial picture brighter.

What is your current monthly income from your job?

____

What is the new "side job"?

____

What are the income and/or goal?

____

What are your new education/training goals?

____

____

____

____

CHAPTER 3
EVALUATE YOUR DEBT

Mortgage – ____________________________________

Car payment -__________________________________

Credit Cards – _________________________________

Personal Loans – _______________________________

Medical/Hospital Bills – ___________________________

Entertainment Expense - __________________________

Other – _______________________________________

Reference free credit reports:

Annualcreditreport.com

CreditKarma.com

Experian.com

Transunion.com

Equifax.com

CHAPTER 4
CREATE A MONTHLY FINANCIAL PLAN (BUDGET)

Complete the Monthly Finances (Budget) pages that are printed in Chapter Four.

Remember to download the full- size copies at: bit.ly/springfinances18

CHAPTER 5
SAVINGS AND EMERGENCY FUND

What could you comfortably save each month? ________

Savings account balance after

6 months____________

12 months___________

3 years______________

5 years______________

Savings account monthly goal______________

Current Savings account info:

Bank

____

Account Number

____

Co-owner or Authorized Signer:

____

Co-owner or Authorized Signer Contact Info:

Address____

Phone____

Chapter 6
Investments

Where have you invested your hard-earned dollars? Be sure to list account/policy numbers and banks/companies and value of your accounts/policies.

- Bank Products ______________________________
- Stocks ______________________________
- Bonds ______________________________
- Investment funds:
    - Mutual funds ______________________________
    - Closed-end funds______________________________
    - Exchange-traded funds______________________________
- Annuities
    - Immediate ______________________________
    - Deferred ______________________________
- Life insurance
    - Term life ______________________________
    - Whole life ______________________________
    - Universal life policies.______________________________
- Retirement
    - 401(k) ______________________________
    - IRA ______________________________

CHAPTER 7
RETIREMENT

Retirement accounts

- Dividends from stocks
- Social Security Income
- Personal Savings
- Small Business income
- Real Estate Investment Income
- IRA or 401K Income

CHAPTER 8
LIFE INSURANCE

Record your current life insurance policy information below.

- Life insurance carrier
- Type of policy
- Policy number
- Coverage amount
- Payment due date
- Monthly/Quarterly payment amount
- Beneficiary

Chapter 9
Your Living Will and Last Will & Testament

Do you have a living will/will?________________________

Who is named as the executor of your estate?

____

Name of guardian for any minor or dependent children:

____

What do you have that you would want to leave to someone?

Use the Notes Section at the back of the book to create a comprehensive list that includes the following information, so the executor can be sure to fulfill your wishes for your beneficiaries.

- Who?
- How much? Or what?
- Where is it?

Chapter 10

Health Check-Up – Body, Mind and Soul

Health goals:

____

____

____

Primary Physician:____________________________

Last Appointment:____________________________

Dentist:____________________________________

Last Appointment:____________________________

Specialist:__________________________________

Appointment (if needed):________________________

NOTES SECTION

For additional copies of the Chapter Check-Up section of this book, go to:

http://bit.ly/EmpowerYourFinancialFuture

ABOUT THE AUTHOR

Cherese Pendleton is the owner of Pendleton Wealth Consultants, a company formed out of the real-life financial experiences she was faced with in 2017.

The first challenge was to help her family plan her brother's funeral. Later in the year the challenge of preparing for loss of wages due to a layoff with her employer. Having only one stream of income Cherese had to prepare a budget for a severance package while looking for work.

With her background in real estate sales and years of experience in the financial services industry, Cherese is passionate about helping women to achieve economic empowerment.

For more information please visit: http://pendletonwealthconsultants.com

Made in the USA
Monee, IL
04 November 2026

67375668R00046